Oh! My Phonics

3

Long Vowels

CEDUBOOK

INTRODUCTION

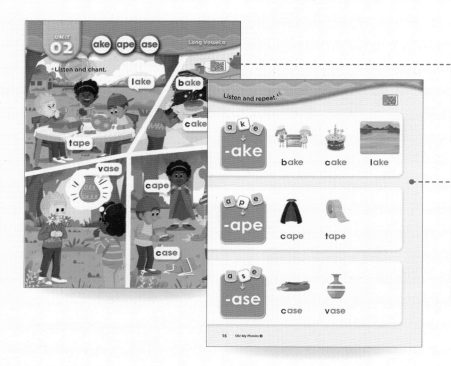

• WORD CHANT

The fun chants and captivating illustrations introduce the target sounds and words.

• LISTEN & REPEAT

Students can learn and practice the target sounds and words. They can also understand the letter-sound relationships.

• WORD READING

Students can practice reading words with the target sounds.

• WRITING

The target sounds and words can be strengthened through writing activities.

• LISTENING

Students can reinforce the target sounds and words through listening activities.

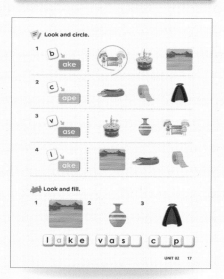

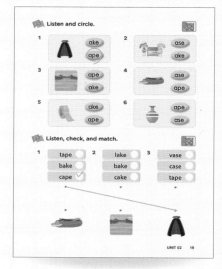

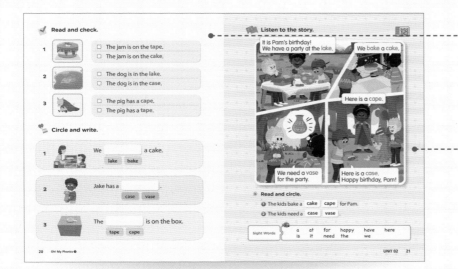

SENTENCE READING

Students can practice reading sentences with the target words.

STORY READING

A phonics story offers students practice with reading target words in natural contexts. They can naturally improve their sight word reading skills.

UNIT QUIZ

Students can check what they have learned in the previous two units.

REVIEW

A variety of activities can help students recall and further practice the sounds and words from previous units.

WORKBOOK

Students can reinforce what they have learned by completing the follow-up exercises featured in the accompanying workbook.

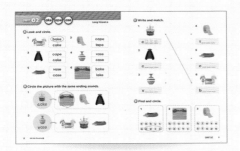

CONTENTS

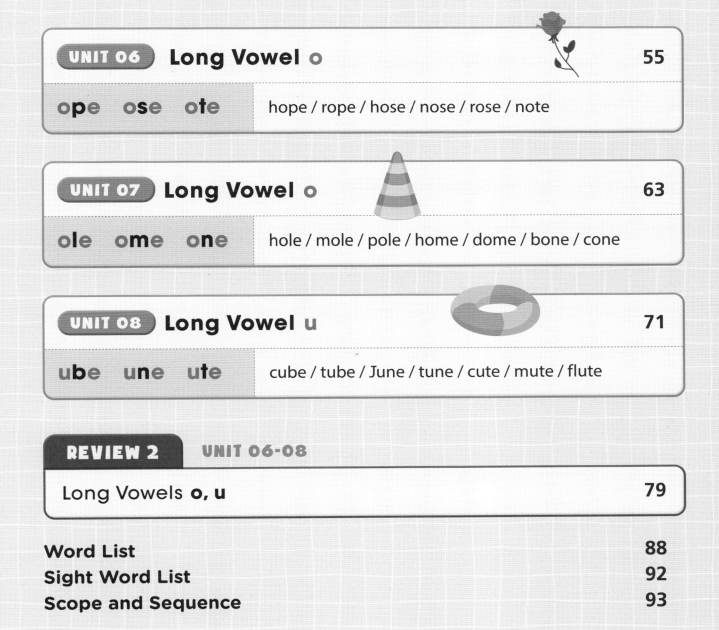

Listen and chant.

a

ham	bag	map	sad	fan

e

bed	pen	ten	vet	wet

i

pin	lip	kid	sit	six

o

dog	log	hot	box	fox

u

rug	run	cup	mud	nut

Look and circle.

1
mad

(mud)

2
wig

wag

3
fix

fox

4
bag

bug

Circle the pictures that rhyme.

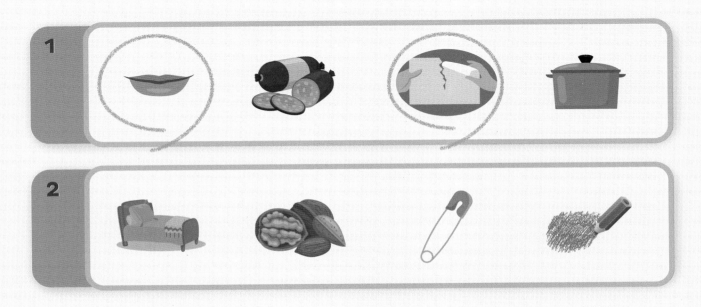

Look, circle, and write.

1 **6** g a b (s i x) e _____ *six*

x s a d i a p

2 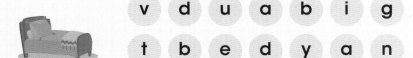 v d u a b i g _____

t b e d y a n

3 c a j a t k t _____

m a t n e a m

4 s a t s u n d _____

t b a f e k l

5 h a p e n k e _____

t b h o t a d

6 r a b u h u g _____

e b a k b i n

7 p o t a t k e _____

s b w q c a p

Listen and match.

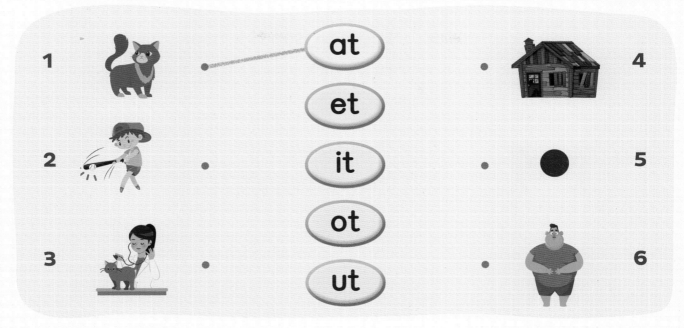

 Listen and choose the rhyming word.

Read and check.

1
☐ The **hen** is in the **tub**.
☑ The **kid** is in the **tub**.

2
☐ I have a **big pen**.
☐ I have a **big fan**.

3
☐ The **man** has a **cup**.
☐ The **man** has a **dog**.

 Circle and write.

1
I ⟨ cut ⟩ ham.
(cut)   mix

2
Ted is a _____ .
kid   vet

3
The dogs _____ on the log.
win   run

Listen to the story.

Let's go to the farm!
There is a ram. There is a cat.
The cat has a nap on the mat.

There are ten hens.
They are red.

1, 2,
... 10!

Zzz

There is a bug on the dog.
There is a big pig.

They live in the hut.
They are happy!

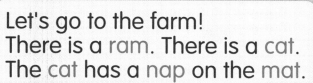

☀ **Read and circle.**

❶ The [**ram**] [**cat**] has a nap.

❷ There is a [**bug**] [**hen**] on the dog.

Sight Words | a   are   go   happy   has   in   is   let's
live   on   the   there   they   to

QUIZ UNIT 01

A Listen and circle.

1

2

B Listen and check.

1 ☐ dog ☑ dad   2 ☐ fix ☐ fan

3 ☐ tub ☐ tag   4 ☐ bud ☐ box

C Look, find, and circle.

1   2

3   4

f	b	a	g	p
n	o	u	h	k
a	b	n	a	i
p	a	n	u	d
q	p	e	n	s

• Listen and chant.

bake **cake** **lake**

cape **tape**

case **vase**

Look and circle.

1 b → **ake**

2 c → **ape**

3 v → **ase**

4 l → **ake**

Look and fill.

1

2

3

l a k e   v a s   c   p

Say, match, and write.

1   t •   • ake
    b •   • ape   *bake*

2   c •   • ake
    t •   • ape

3   l •   • ake
    b •   • ave

4   c •   • ave
    w •   • ake

5   v •   • ase
    b •   • ape

6   w •   • ake
    t •   • ape

7   b •   • ase
    c •   • ape

Listen and circle.

1

ake

ape

2

ase

ake

3

ape

ake

4

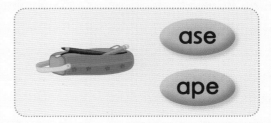

ase

ape

5

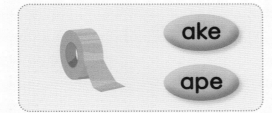

ake

ape

6

ape

ase

 Listen, check, and match.

1
tape ◯
bake ◯
cape ✓

2
lake ◯
bake ◯
cake ◯

3
vase ◯
case ◯
tape ◯

Read and check.

1
☐ The jam is on the **tape**.
☐ The jam is on the **cake**.

2
☐ The dog is in the **lake**.
☐ The dog is in the **case**.

3
☐ The pig has a **cape**.
☐ The pig has a **tape**.

 Circle and write.

1
We _____ a cake.
lake　bake

2
Jake has a _____ .
case　vase

3
The _____ is on the box.
tape　cape

Listen to the story.

☀ **Read and circle.**

❶ The kids bake a | cake | cape | for Pam.

❷ The kids need a | case | vase | .

Sight Words	a at for happy have here
	is it need the we

QUIZ UNIT 02

A Listen and circle.

1

2

B Listen and check.

1 ☐ vase ☐ case

2 ☐ cape ☐ tape

3 ☐ bake ☐ lake

4 ☐ case ☐ cake

C Look, find, and circle.

1

2

3

4

f	v	c	a	p
t	a	p	e	l
a	s	n	k	a
p	e	p	a	k
h	c	a	s	e

Listen and chant.

date

name

Sam

Sam

same

cave

wave

late

gate

name same

date gate late

cave wave

Look and circle.

1

w → **ave**

2

d → **ate**

3

n → **ame**

4

l → **ate**

Look and fill.

1 **2** **3**

g □ t e   s a m □   c □ v □

Say, match, and write.

1 　l •　　• ate　_____

　　　　　　　b •　　• ame　_____

2 　d •　　• ave　_____

　　　　　　　s •　　• ame　_____

3 　c •　　• ate　_____

　　　　　　　n •　　• ave　_____

4 　s •　　• ate　_____

　　　　　　　g •　　• ame　_____

5 　c •　　• ave　_____

　　　　　　　w •　　• ate　_____

6 　d •　　• ame　_____

　　　　　　　n •　　• ate　_____

7 Kate　n •　　• ave　_____

　　　　　　　l •　　• ame　_____

Listen and circle.

1

ate
ame

2

ame
ave

3
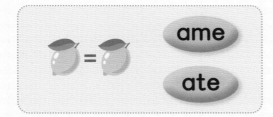
ame
ate

4
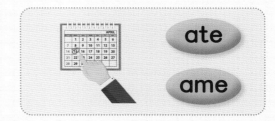
ate
ame

5

ave
ame

6

ate
ave

 Listen, check, and match.

1
date ◯
gate ◯
late ◯

2
cave ◯
late ◯
wave ◯

3
same ◯
name ◯
cave ◯

Read and check.

1
- ☐ We have the **same name**.
- ☐ We have the **same date**.

2
- ☐ It is a big **wave**.
- ☐ It is a big **gate**.

3
- ☐ The cat is in the **wave**.
- ☐ The cat is in the **cave**.

 Circle and write.

1  The _____ is big.

cave   gate

2  Mike is _____ .

gate   late

3  My _____ is Kate.

same   name

Listen to the story.

We are friends.
We have the same name.
And we have the same birthday.

We play in the cave.
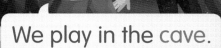

We play in the wave.

We meet at the gate.
Oh no! I am late!

☀ **Read and circle.**

1 They have the same name birthday.

2 They play in the gate cave .

| Sight Words | am   and   are   at   have   I   in   no   oh |
| | play   the   we |

QUIZ UNIT 02-03

A Listen and circle.

1

2

B Listen and check.

1
☐ lake ☐ gate

2
☐ case ☐ cave

3
☐ vase ☐ wave

4
☐ tape ☐ cape

C Look, find, and circle.

1

2

Kate

3

4

n	d	a	t	e
n	a	a	h	p
a	m	m	a	a
c	a	p	e	t
h	b	a	k	e

Listen and chant.

hide

ride

wide

bike

hike

line

nine

pine

Look and circle.

1

hike

bike

2

line

nine

3
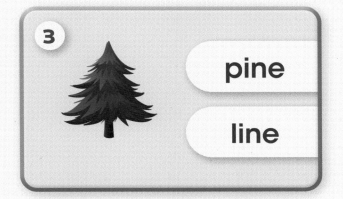

pine

line

4

hide

hike

Circle the pictures that rhyme.

Look, circle, and write.

1 c a b i t k e _____

   t b i k e a m _____

2 l i b a t k k _____

   n l i h i d e _____

3 f g y u t k w _____

   x b h i k e h _____

4 w a b w i d e _____

   t w i k e e p _____

5 j i n e t k c _____

   q m b l i n e _____

6 c p i n e k l _____

   o b a k e a u _____

7 c a b a t k y _____

   p r i d e a q _____

Listen and match.

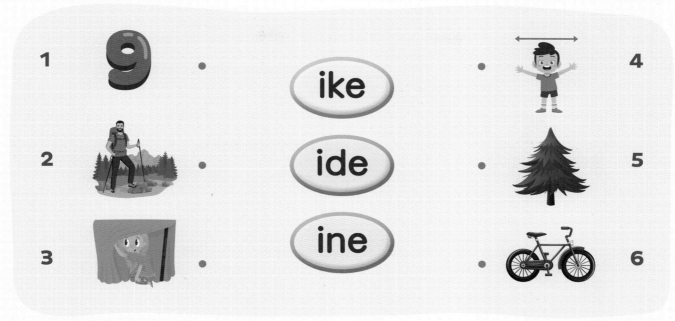

1 9

2

3

ike

ide

ine

4

5

6

 Listen and choose the rhyming word.

1 a b c

2 a b c

3 a b c

Read and check.

1
☐ **Nine lines** are on the box.
☐ **Nine lines** are on the mat.

2
☐ The kid **rides** a **bike**.
☐ The kid **hides** a **bike**.

3
☐ The man **hikes** to the **pine**.
☐ The man **rides** to the **pine**.

 Circle and write.

1
It is a _____ bed.

pine wide

2
The kids _____ in the cave.

hide ride

3
The bugs are on the _____ .

nine line

Listen to the story.

My name is Mike.
I like to hike.

1. 2.
...9!

There are nine pines
on the top.
I hike to the pines.

I like to ride a bike, too.

FINISH

Ted and I ride a bike.
Look! There is a finish line!

☀ **Read and circle.**

❶ Mike likes to | hike | hide |.

❷ Ted and Mike | line | ride | a bike.

QUIZ UNIT 03-04

A Listen and circle.

1

2

B Listen and check.

1 ☐ cave ☐ wave   2 ☐ nine ☐ pine

3 ☐ hide ☐ ride   4 ☐ date ☐ late

C Look, find, and circle.

1   2

3   4

s	d	c	w	p
j	a	p	i	e
a	s	m	d	a
g	a	t	e	t
h	i	k	e	j

UNIT 05

ice ite ive

Long Vowel i

Listen and chant.

-ice

dice

mice

-ite

bite

kite

-ive

dive

five

hive

Look and circle.

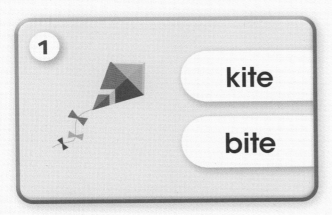

1. kite / bite

2. dice / mice

3. dive / dice

4. hive / five

Circle the pictures that rhyme.

Look, circle, and write.

1 c a b i t e e
t b i k e a m
_____

2 g i p a u k p
x l i h i v e
_____

3 m i c e i c a
y b a c k a t
_____

4 b g k i t e o
w b g i k e h
_____

5 w a b w i d e
m i f i v e p
_____

6 o i d i c e c
d i v e i n e
_____

7 g a t e t k z
k i d i v e z
_____

Listen and match.

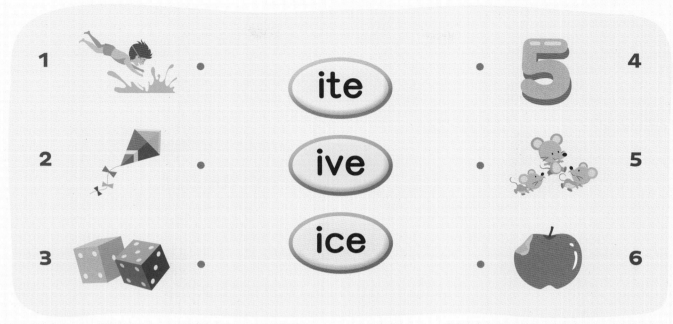

1

2

3

ite

ive

ice

4

5

6

 Listen and choose the rhyming word.

1 a b c

2 a b c

3 a b c

Read and check.

1

☐ The **hive** is on the pine.

☐ The **kite** is on the pine.

2

☐ **Five mice** are in the box.

☐ **Five dice** are in the box.

3

☐ The kids **dive** in the lake.

☐ The kids **bite** in the lake.

 Circle and write.

1  The kid has a big _____ .

kite   dice

2  The mice _____ nuts.

dive   bite

3  _____ pigs are in the mud.

Hive   Five

Listen to the story.

* **Read and circle.**

1 They like to fly a [**kite** **hive**].

2 Mike has the [**mice** **dice**].

Sight Words a has have in let's like the to we

QUIZ UNIT 04-05

A Listen and circle.

1

2

B Listen and check.

1 ☐ hike ☐ hive   2 ☐ dive ☐ dice

3 ☐ bite ☐ ride   4 ☐ hide ☐ wide

C Look, find, and circle.

1    2

3    4

b	z	k	e	p
f	i	v	e	i
a	i	m	d	n
d	b	i	k	e
m	i	c	e	j

Check the words you can read.
Then listen and repeat.

Long Vowel a

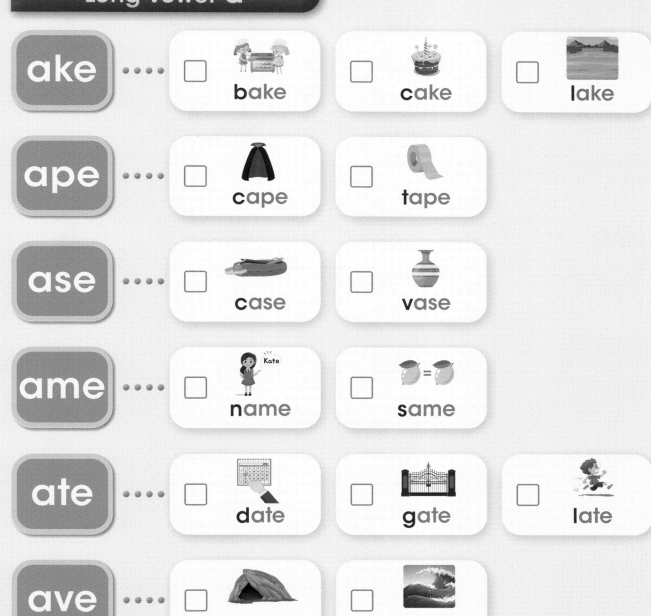

ake ·····
- ☐ bake
- ☐ cake
- ☐ lake

ape ·····
- ☐ cape
- ☐ tape

ase ·····
- ☐ case
- ☐ vase

ame ·····
- ☐ name
- ☐ same

ate ·····
- ☐ date
- ☐ gate
- ☐ late

ave ·····
- ☐ cave
- ☐ wave

Check the words you can read.
Then listen and repeat.

Long Vowel i

ide ····
- ☐ hide
- ☐ ride
- ☐ wide

ike ····
- ☐ bike
- ☐ hike

ine ····
- ☐ line
- ☐ nine
- ☐ pine

ice ····
- ☐ dice
- ☐ mice

ite ····
- ☐ bite
- ☐ kite

ive ····
- ☐ dive
- ☐ five
- ☐ hive

A Listen and circle.

B Listen, circle, and check.

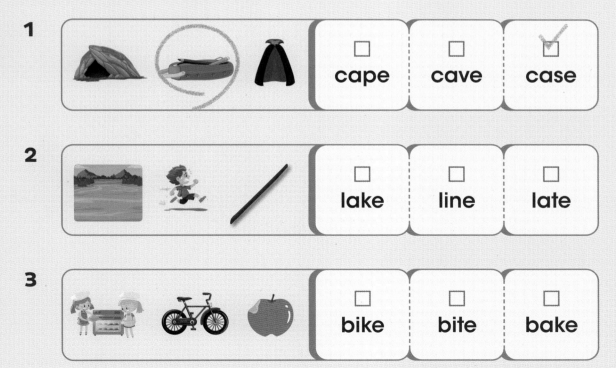

1

☐ cape   ☐ cave   ☑ case

2

☐ lake   ☐ line   ☐ late

3

☐ bike   ☐ bite   ☐ bake

C **Look and circle.**

1

(gate)

date

2

hive

hide

3

dive

dice

D **Find, color, and write.**

1

(a) (i)

c_a_ke

2

(a) (i)

f___ve

3

(a) (i)

v___se

4

(a) (i)

m___ce

5

(a) (i)

t___pe

6

(a) (i)

p___ne

Listen and check.

1

2

3

4

Listen and circle.

1 A name is on the  .

2 Jake and I like to  .

3 The is wide.

4 A gate is in the   .

G Find the rhyming words and write the numbers.

ape   3,

ine

ase

ice

H What does not rhyme? Find and cross out.

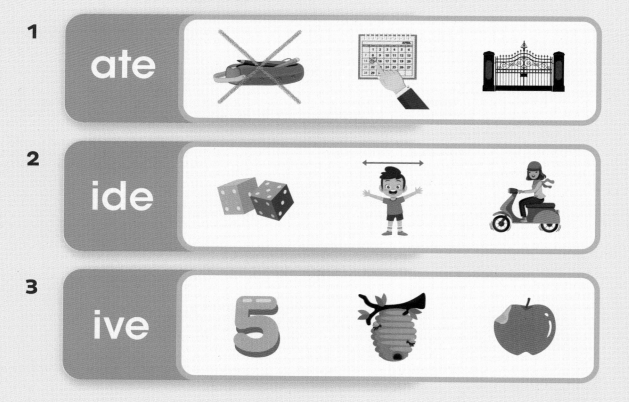

1 ate

2 ide

3 ive

1 Look and write.

1

The kids ___dive___ in the ___lake___ .

2

The _____ is by the _____ .

3

We have the _____ _____ .

4

The _____ has six _____ s.

5

We _____ in the _____ .

J Write the words in the correct column.

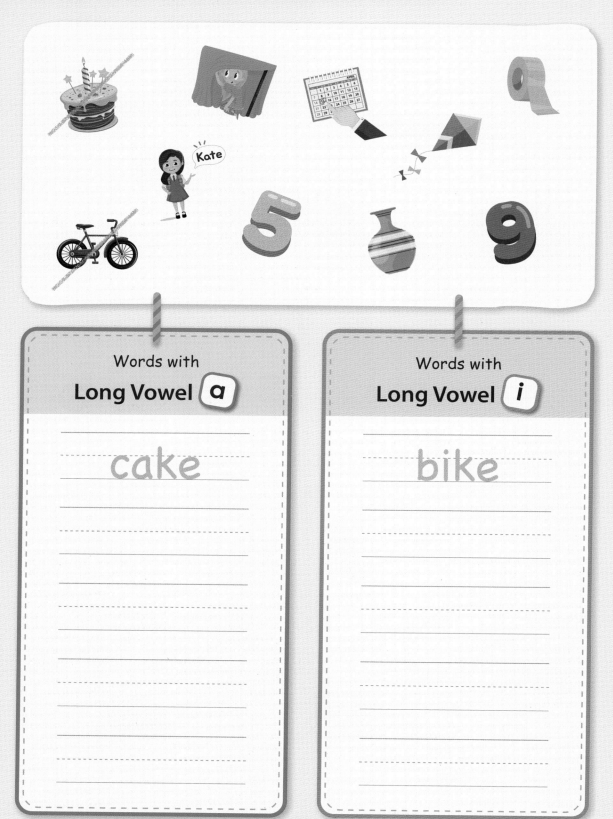

Words with
Long Vowel a

cake
_____
_____
_____
_____
_____
_____
_____

Words with
Long Vowel i

bike
_____
_____
_____
_____
_____
_____
_____

Listen and chant.

hope

rope

hose

nose

rose

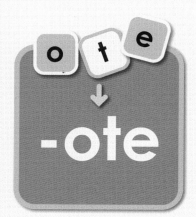

note

Look and circle.

1

h → **ose**

2

r → **ope**

3

n → **ote**

Look and fill.

1   **2**   **3**

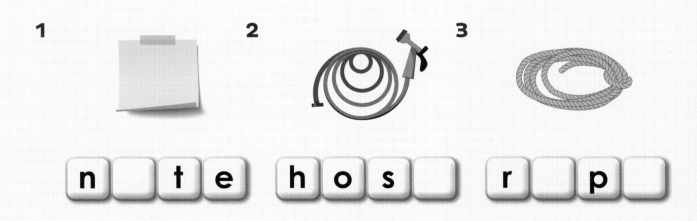

n [ ] t e   h o s [ ]   r [ ] p [ ]

Say, match, and write.

1 　r •　　• | ose |　　_____

　　　　　　t •　　• | ope |

2 　n •　　• | ote |　　_____

　　　　　　b •　　• | ose |

3 　m •　　• | ote |　　_____

　　　　　　n •　　• | ope |

4 　h •　　• | ose |　　_____

　　　　　　n •　　• | ote |

5 　r •　　• | ote |　　_____

　　　　　　c •　　• | ose |

6 　n •　　• | ote |　　_____

　　　　　　h •　　• | ope |

Listen and circle.

1
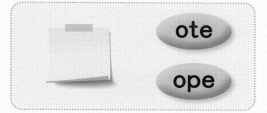
ote
ope

2

ote
ose

3
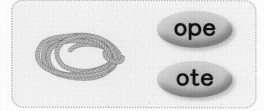
ope
ote

4

ose
ope

5
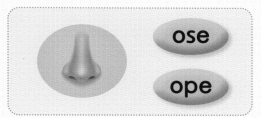
ose
ope

6

ope
ose

 ## Listen, check, and match.

1
hope ◯
hose ◯
nose ◯

2
rose ◯
nose ◯
note ◯

3
rope ◯
rose ◯
hope ◯

•   •   •

Read and check.

1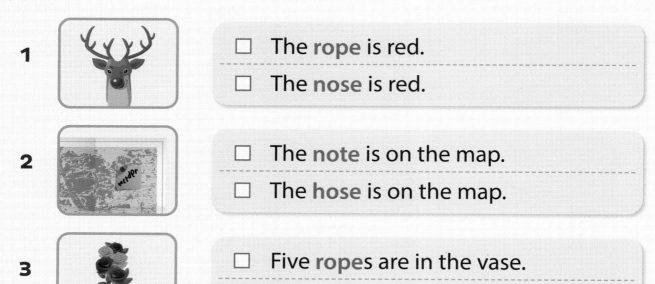

☐ The **rope** is red.

☐ The **nose** is red.

2

☐ The **note** is on the map.

☐ The **hose** is on the map.

3

☐ Five **rope**s are in the vase.

☐ Five **rose**s are in the vase.

 Circle and write.

1  A bug is on the _____ .

note   nose

2 The _____ is on the bag.

rope   hope

3 The cat is on the _____ .

rose   hose

Listen to the story.

☀ **Read and circle.**

1 She wants a [**rose**] [**hose**] garden.

2 She smells the roses with her [**note**] [**nose**] .

Sight Words ▷ a have I is look love my the this want with

QUIZ **UNIT 05-06**

A Listen and circle.

1

2

B Listen and check.

1 ☐ rope   ☐ rose

2 ☐ five   ☐ dive

3 ☐ note   ☐ kite

4 ☐ mice   ☐ dice

C Look, find, and circle.

1   2

3   4

n	o	s	e	w
h	b	d	o	j
i	m	i	s	a
v	a	p	t	l
e	n	o	t	e

• **Listen and chant.**

mole

hole

pole

dome

cone

bone

home

hole

mole

pole

home

dome

bone

cone

Look and circle.

1 h → ole

2 d → ome

3 b → one

4 m → ole

Look and fill.

1    **2**    **3**

c ☐ n e   d o m ☐   p ☐ l ☐

Say, match, and write.

1   d •   • ole   _____

    h •   • ome   _____

2   d •   • ole   _____

    p •   • one   _____

3   m •   • ole   _____

    h •   • one   _____

4   c •   • one   _____

    g •   • ome   _____

5   b •   • ole   _____

    n •   • one   _____

6   n •   • one   _____

    m •   • ole   _____

7   h •   • ole   _____

    p •   • ome   _____

Listen and circle.

1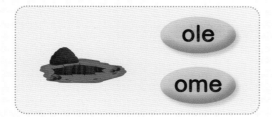

ole

ome

2

ome

one

3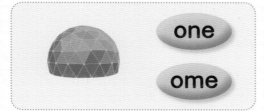

one

ome

4

ole

ome

5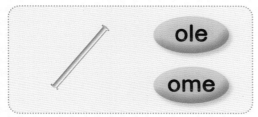

ole

ome

6

ole

one

 Listen, check, and match.

1
cone

dome

bone

2
hole

pole

mole

3
home

dome

hole

Read and check.

1

☐ The **mole** is in the **hole**.

☐ The **mole** is in the **cone**.

2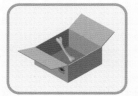

☐ The **cone** is in the box.

☐ The **bone** is in the box.

3

☐ The **hole** is on the cape.

☐ The **pole** is on the cape.

 ## Circle and write.

1

There are five _____ s.

mole   pole

2

The dome has a _____ .

pole   hole

3

My dog is at _____ .

dome   home

Listen to the story.

Sam and Jane are moles.
They want a home.
They make a hole.

Sam has a pole.
Jane has a dome.

Sam has a cone.
Jane has a bone.

Wow! It is a nice home.

✳ **Read and circle.**

❶ Sam and Jane make a dome home .

❷ Jane has a pole bone .

Sight Words	a	and	are	has	is	it	make
	nice	they	are	want	wow		

QUIZ UNIT 06-07

A Listen and circle.

1

2

B Listen and check.

1 ☐ hose ☐ home

2 ☐ rope ☐ mole

3 ☐ hope ☐ hole

4 ☐ note ☐ bone

C Look, find, and circle.

1

2

3

4

n	d	s	a	e
r	a	o	h	r
o	m	o	a	o
p	l	p	e	s
e	b	o	n	e

• **Listen and chant.**

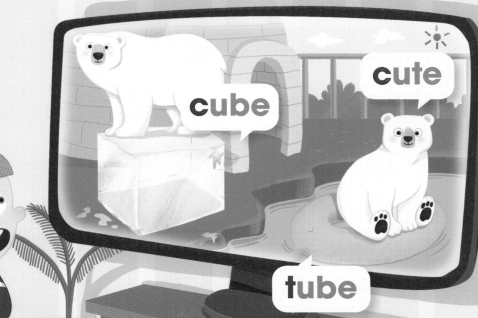

June

cube

cute

tube

tune

flute

mute

cube   **tube**

June   **tune**

cute   **mute**   **flute**

Look and circle.

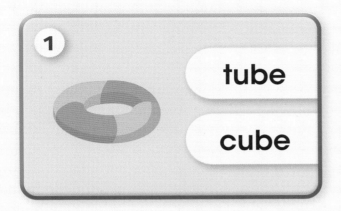

1. tube / cube

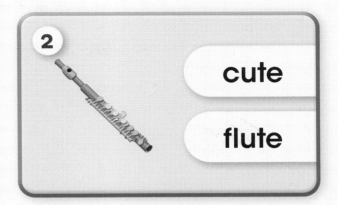

2. cute / flute

3. mute / cute

4. June / tune

Circle the pictures that rhyme.

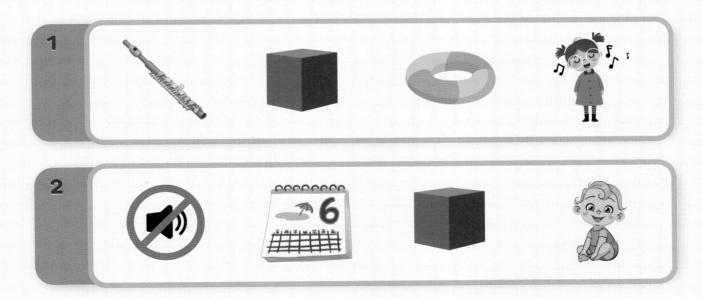

Look, circle, and write.

1

c u b e o a p

f o u w e a l

_____

2

f l u t e c a

m b a c k a t

_____

3

q g k i t e o

t u b e k e h

_____

4

j a b w i d e

t u n e i g p

_____

5

c i d e t k c

d i c u t e e

_____

6

d r i n e k l

m u t e i c e

_____

7

k i J u n e u

J i d e e a d

_____

Listen and match.

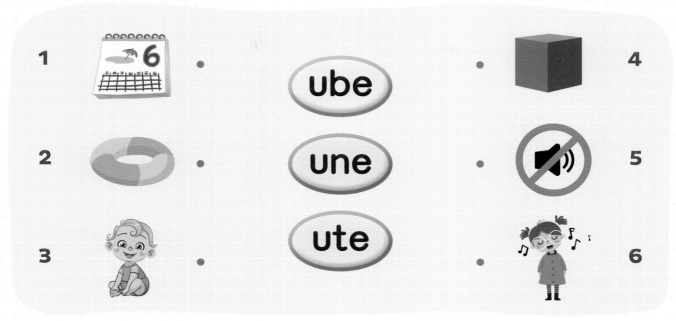

1   ube   4

2   une   5

3   ute   6

 ## Listen and choose the rhyming word.

1

2

3

Read and check.

1

☐ A **cube** is in the tub.

☐ A **tube** is in the tub.

2

☐ Kate makes a **tune**.

☐ Kate is **mute**.

3

☐ A red bug is on the **flute**.

☐ A red bug is on the **cube**.

 Circle and write.

1  It's hot in _____.

June   tune

2  They cut the _____.

flute   cube

3  A _____ cat is in the mud.

tube   cute

Look! A bear is on a cube.
A bear is on a tube.
They are cute.

A man plays the flute.
I like the tune.

I can't hear the tune.
Oh! It is my dog Duke!

✳ **Read and circle.**

❶ Two bears are on the cube.　　Yes　No

❷ The man plays the flute.　　Yes　No

Sight Words	a	are	can't	I	is	it	like	look
	my	oh	on	plays	the	they		

QUIZ UNIT 07-08

A Listen and circle.

1

2

B Listen and check.

1 ☐ bone ☐ cone

2 ☐ flute ☐ mute

3 ☐ cube ☐ tube

4 ☐ mole ☐ pole

C Look, find, and circle.

1   **2**

3  **4**

d	o	m	e	d
h	o	l	e	m
q	o	t	d	o
t	u	n	e	l
c	i	c	e	e

Check the words you can read. Then listen and repeat.

Long Vowel o

ope · · · · ·
- [ ]  hope
- [ ]  rope

ose · · · · ·
- [ ]  hose
- [ ] 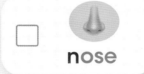 nose
- [ ]  rose

ote · · · · ·
- [ ]  note

ole · · · · ·
- [ ] 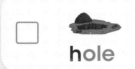 hole
- [ ] 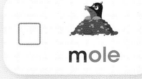 mole
- [ ]  pole

ome · · · · ·
- [ ]  home
- [ ] 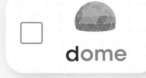 dome

one · · · · ·
- [ ] 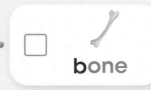 bone
- [ ]  cone

Check the words you can read. Then listen and repeat.

Long Vowel u

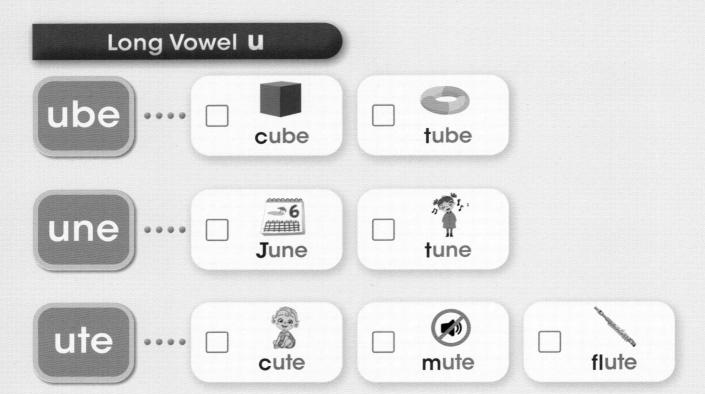

ube ···· ☐ cube   ☐ tube

une ···· ☐ June   ☐ tune

ute ···· ☐ cute   ☐ mute   ☐ flute

A   Listen and circle.

1

2

3

4

B   Listen, circle, and check.

1

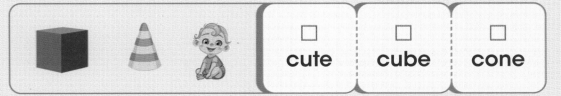

☐ hose	☑ hope	☐ hole

2

☐ cute	☐ cube	☐ cone

C **Look and circle.**

1

hope

rope

2

cube

tube

3

cute

flute

D **Find, color, and write.**

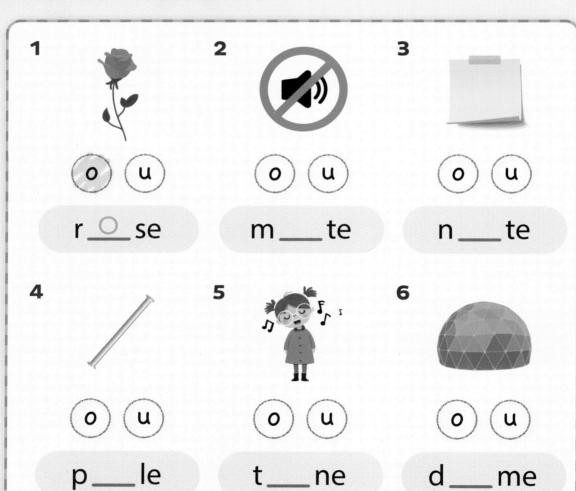

1 (o) (u)

r__o__se

2 (o) (u)

m___te

3 (o) (u)

n___te

4 (o) (u)

p___le

5 (o) (u)

t___ne

6 (o) (u)

d___me

E **Listen and check.**

1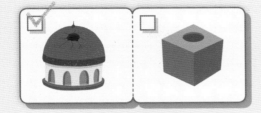

2

3

4

F **Listen and circle.**

1 The  is cute.

2 The   is in the box.

3 The man has a red   .

4 The mole is in the   .

G Find the rhyming words and write the numbers.

ose
2,

ube

ole

une

H What does not rhyme? Find and cross out.

ome

ute

one

I Look and write.

1

I see _____rose_____ s in _____June_____ .

2

The _____ is on the _____ .

3

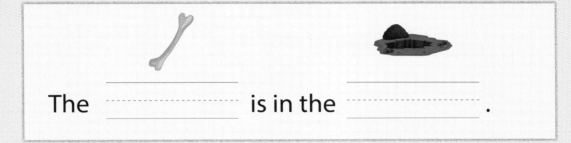

The _____ is in the _____ .

4

The _____ s go _____ .

5

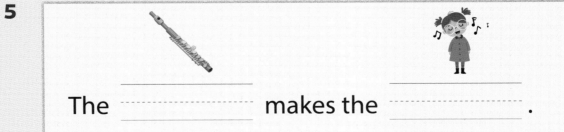

The _____ makes the _____ .

J **Write the words in the correct column.**

Words with Long Vowel **o**	Words with Long Vowel **u**
bone	mute

WORD LIST

- Can you read? Read and check.

UNIT 01

1. ☐ cat
2. ☐ ram
3. ☐ mat
4. ☐ nap
5. ☐ red
6. ☐ hen
7. ☐ ten
8. ☐ big
9. ☐ pig
10. ☐ dog
11. ☐ bug
12. ☐ sun
13. ☐ hut

UNIT 02

14. ☐ bake
15. ☐ cake
16. ☐ lake
17. ☐ cape
18. ☐ tape
19. ☐ case
20. ☐ vase

UNIT 03

21	☐		name
22	☐		same
23	☐		date
24	☐		gate
25	☐		late
26	☐		cave
27	☐		wave

UNIT 04

28	☐	hide
29	☐	ride
30	☐	wide
31	☐	bike
32	☐	hike
33	☐	line
34	☐	nine
35	☐	pine

WORD LIST

• Can you read? Read and check.

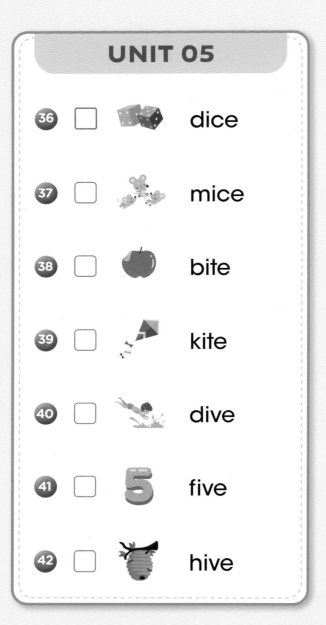

UNIT 05

36 ☐ dice

37 ☐ mice

38 ☐ bite

39 ☐ kite

40 ☐ dive

41 ☐ five

42 ☐ hive

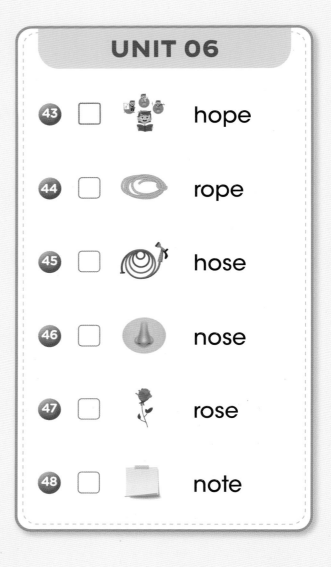

UNIT 06

43 ☐ hope

44 ☐ rope

45 ☐ hose

46 ☐ nose

47 ☐ rose

48 ☐ note

UNIT 07

49	☐	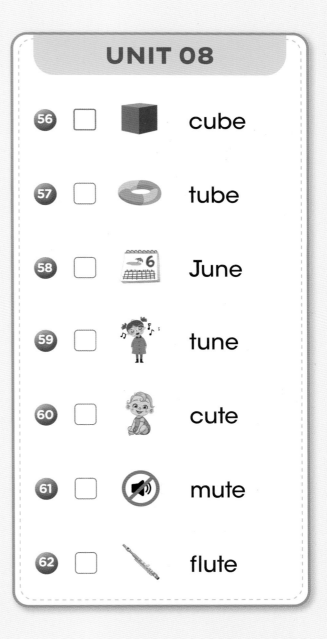	hole
50	☐		mole
51	☐		pole
52	☐		home
53	☐		dome
54	☐		bone
55	☐		cone

UNIT 08

56	☐	cube
57	☐	tube
58	☐	June
59	☐	tune
60	☐	cute
61	☐	mute
62	☐	flute

SIGHT WORD LIST

• **Can you read? Read and check.**

#		Word	Pages
1	☐	a	13, 21, 37, 45, 61, 69
2	☐	am	29
3	☐	and	29, 37, 69
4	☐	are	13, 29, 37, 69
5	☐	at	21, 29
6	☐	for	21
7	☐	go	13
8	☐	happy	13, 21
9	☐	has	13, 45, 77
10	☐	have	21, 29, 45, 61
11	☐	here	21
12	☐	I	29, 37, 61
13	☐	in	13, 29, 45
14	☐	is	13, 21, 37, 61, 77
15	☐	it	21, 77
16	☐	let's	13, 45
17	☐	like	37, 45
18	☐	live	13
19	☐	look	37, 61
20	☐	love	61
21	☐	make	77
22	☐	my	37, 61
23	☐	need	21
24	☐	nice	77
25	☐	no	29
26	☐	oh	29
27	☐	on	13, 37
28	☐	play	29
29	☐	the	13, 21, 29, 37, 45, 61
30	☐	there	13, 37
31	☐	they	13, 77
32	☐	this	61
33	☐	to	13, 37, 45
34	☐	too	37
35	☐	want	61, 77
36	☐	we	21, 29, 45

SCOPE & SEQUENCE

Book 1 — Alphabet Sounds

UNIT 01	Aa Bb Cc
UNIT 02	Dd Ee Ff
UNIT 03	Gg Hh Ii
UNIT 04	Jj Kk Ll
UNIT 05	Mm Nn Oo
UNIT 06	Pp Qq Rr
UNIT 07	Ss Tt Uu Vv
UNIT 08	Ww Xx Yy Zz

Book 2 — Short Vowels

UNIT 01	Short Vowel a: am, ag, ap
UNIT 02	Short Vowel a: ad, an, at
UNIT 03	Short Vowel i: ig, in, ip
UNIT 04	Short Vowel i: id, it, ix
UNIT 05	Short Vowel e: ed, en, et
UNIT 06	Short Vowel o: og, ot, ox
UNIT 07	Short Vowel u: ug, un, up
UNIT 08	Short Vowel u: ub, ud, ut

Book 3 — Long Vowels

UNIT 01	Short Vowels Review
UNIT 02	Long Vowel a: a_e
UNIT 03	Long Vowel a: a_e
UNIT 04	Long Vowel i: i_e
UNIT 05	Long Vowel i: i_e
UNIT 06	Long Vowel o: o_e
UNIT 07	Long Vowel o: o_e
UNIT 08	Long Vowel u: u_e

Book 4 — Double Letters

UNIT 01	Consonant Blends : bl, fl, gl, sl
UNIT 02	Consonant Blends : br, cr, dr, gr
UNIT 03	Consonant Blends : sm, sn, st, sw
UNIT 04	Consonant Digraphs : sh, ch, th, ng
UNIT 05	Vowel Digraphs : ai, ay Vowel Diphthongs : oi, oy
UNIT 06	Vowel Digraphs : oa, ow1 (snow) Vowel Diphthongs : ou, ow2 (cow)
UNIT 07	R-controlled Vowels : ar, or, ir, er
UNIT 08	Vowel Digraphs: ee, ea, short oo, long oo

MEMO

MEMO

Flashcards

with SAYPEN

UNIT 01

UNIT 01

UNIT 01

UNIT 01

UNIT 02

UNIT 01

UNIT 01

UNIT 01

UNIT 02

UNIT 01

UNIT 01

UNIT 01
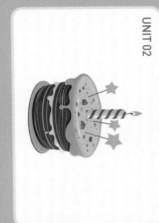

UNIT 02

UNIT 01
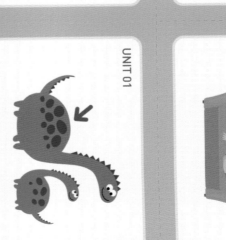

UNIT 01

UNIT 01

Oh! My Phonics

3

Long Vowels

Workbook

CEDU BOOK

CONTENTS

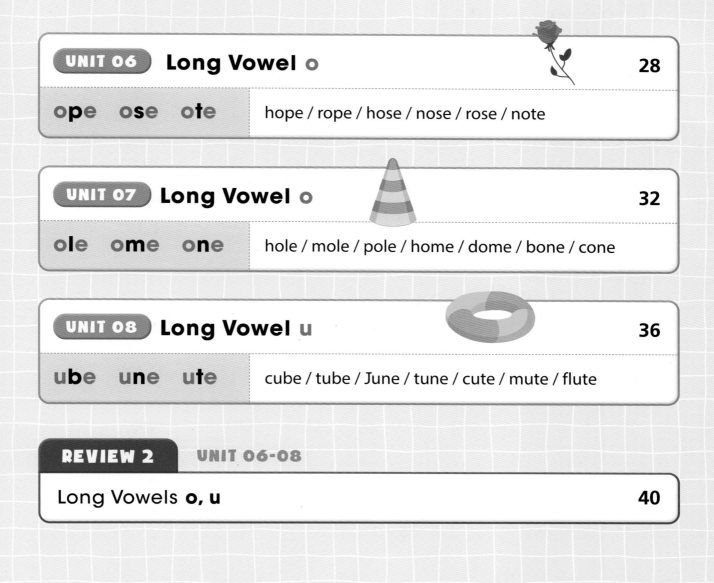

A Circle and write.

1

ap	(at)

m at

2

en	et

v

3

in	ip

l

4

ox	ot

b

5

ig	it

w

6

ug	ut

h

7

am	an

f

8

ed	et

r

9

ot	ox

d

10

en	ed

p

11

ud	un

b

12

ap	an

m

B Write the missing vowel for each word below.

a   e   i   o   u

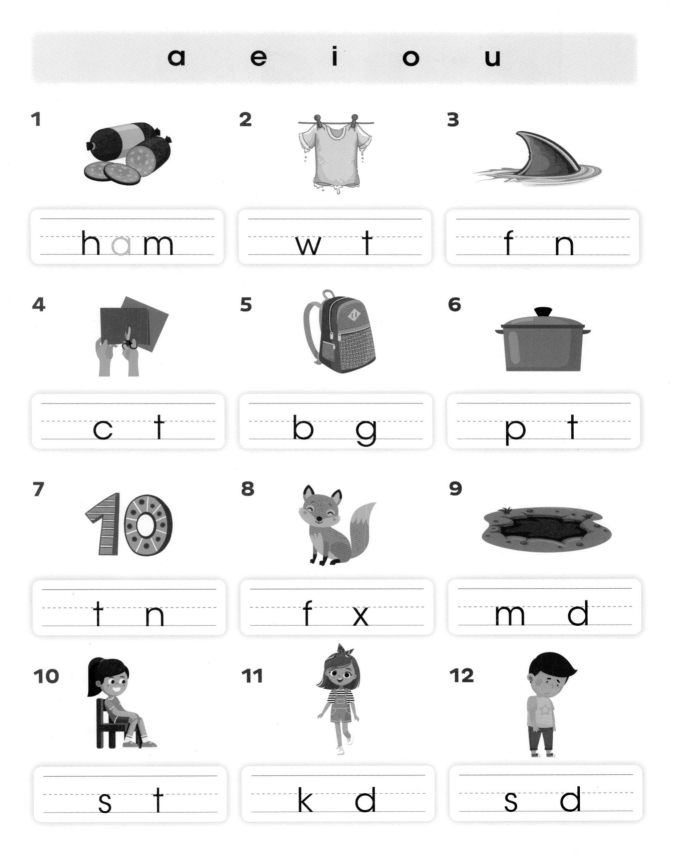

1 h a m

2 w t

3 f n

4 c t

5 b g

6 p t

7 t n

8 f x

9 m d

10 s t

11 k d

12 s d

C Circle the pictures with the matching sound.

1

2

3

4

5

D Do the puzzle.

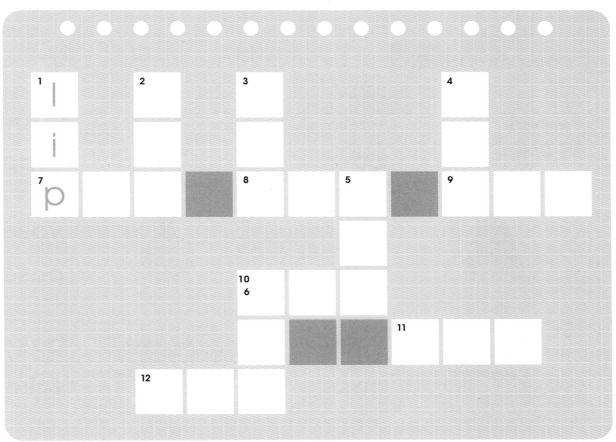

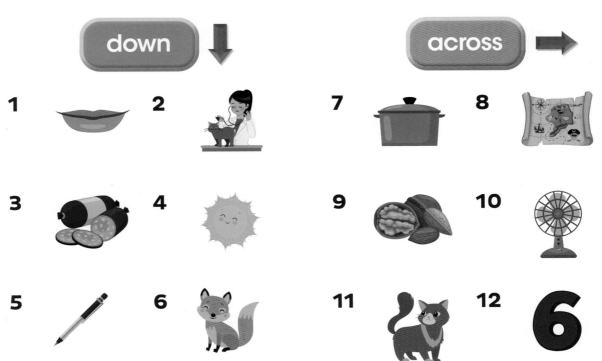

A Look and circle.

1

bake

cake

2

cape

tape

3

cape

cake

4

vase

case

5

vase

case

6

bake

lake

B Circle the picture with the same ending sounds.

1

cake

2

vase

C Write and match.

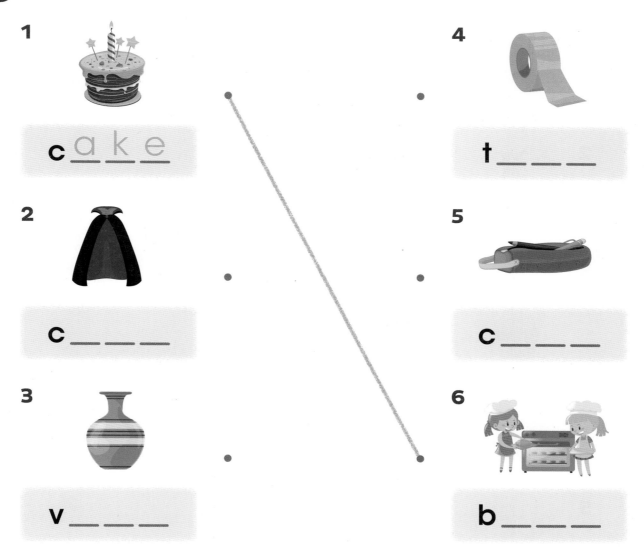

1 c<u>a k e</u>

2 c _ _ _ _

3 v _ _ _ _

4 t _ _ _ _

5 c _ _ _ _

6 b _ _ _ _

D Find and circle.

1

c	a	b	u	s
a	c	a	s	e

2

b	l	a	k	e
v	a	s	h	y

3

h	t	a	k	e
k	t	a	p	e

E Check and write.

1 
☐ -ake
☑ -ape

cape   cape

2 
☐ -ase
☐ -ake

3 
☐ -ape
☐ -ake

4 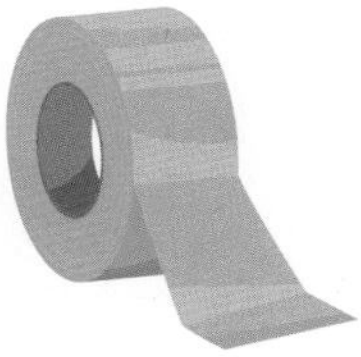
☐ -ase
☐ -ape

5 
☐ -ake
☐ -ape

6 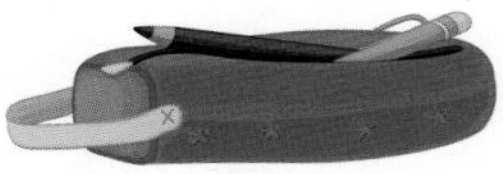
☐ -ape
☐ -ase

7 
☐ -ape
☐ -ake

F **Find, circle, and write.**

c	o	q	b	s	p	v	s
v	d	c	b	a	k	e	k
a	r	a	a	e	g	l	z
s	a	p	c	s	a	a	c
e	p	e	m	s	e	k	f
d	v	f	e	c	v	e	l
t	a	p	e	a	z	a	t
j	w	g	c	a	k	i	d

1 **-ake**

bake

_____

_____

2 **-ape**

_____

_____

_____

3 **-ase**

_____

_____

_____

A Look and circle.

1

gate

wave

2

late

cave

3

same

name

4

name

same

5

gate

date

6

date

late

B Circle the picture with the same ending sounds.

1

wave

2

gate

C Write and match.

1

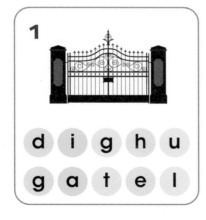

c __ __ __

4

l __ __ __

2

Kate

n __ __ __

5

s __ __ __

3

d __ __ __

6

w __ __ __

D Find and circle.

1

d	i	g	h	u
g	a	t	e	l

2

q	c	a	v	e
p	o	w	b	z

3

Kate

b	v	a	s	e
f	n	a	m	e

E Check and write.

1
- [ ] -ave
- [ ] -ate

2
- [ ] -ame
- [ ] -ave

3
- [ ] -ate
- [ ] -ame

4
- [ ] -ave
- [ ] -ame

5
- [ ] -ave
- [ ] -ate

6
- [ ] -ame
- [ ] -ate

7
- [ ] -ame
- [ ] -ave

F Find, circle, and write.

l	d	v	n	a	f	l	a
a	r	a	c	a	v	e	l
t	a	s	a	m	e	n	w
e	n	e	n	g	x	e	l
d	a	t	e	a	v	k	b
t	a	p	m	v	m	a	h
j	s	a	w	a	v	e	i
e	a	k	z	m	o	q	z

1 -ame

same

2 -ate

3 -ave

A Look and circle.

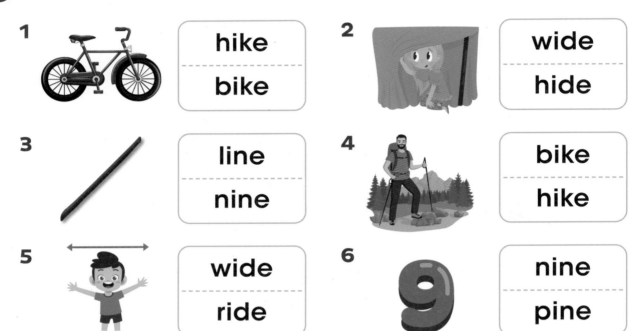

1. hike / bike

2. wide / hide

3. line / nine

4. bike / hike

5. wide / ride

6. nine / pine

B Circle the picture with the same ending sounds.

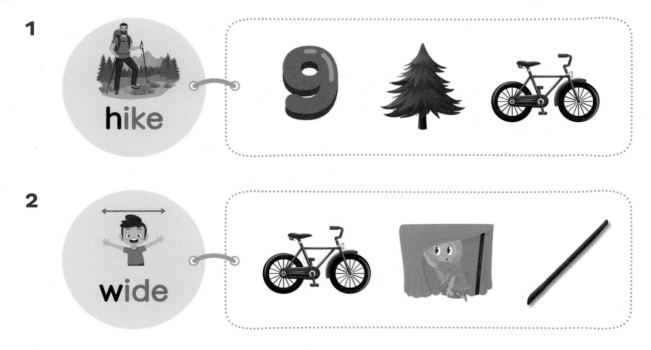

1. hike

2. wide

C Write and match.

1

h_ _ _ _

2

l_ _ _ _

3

w_ _ _ _

4

p_ _ _ _

5

b_ _ _ _

6

h_ _ _ _

D Find and circle.

1

g r i d e
t e p a t

2

i c a k e
h i k e z

3

q w g a v
n i n e o

E Check and write.

1

☐ -ine
☐ -ike

2

☐ -ike
☐ -ide

3

☐ -ine
☐ -ike

4

☐ -ide
☐ -ine

5

☐ -ike
☐ -ine

6

☐ -ide
☐ -ine

7

☐ -ide
☐ -ike

r	l	r	p	h	k	h	f
l	i	w	l	t	z	i	d
m	v	d	h	i	i	k	z
b	m	r	e	o	j	e	l
h	i	z	o	n	i	f	v
i	m	k	l	i	n	e	b
d	m	v	e	n	e	p	e
e	c	h	f	e	x	k	e

1 -ide

ride

2 -ike

3 -ine

A Look and circle.

1

bite
kite

2

mice
dice

3

dice
mice

4

bite
dive

5

dive
five

6

five
hive

B Circle the picture with the same ending sounds.

1

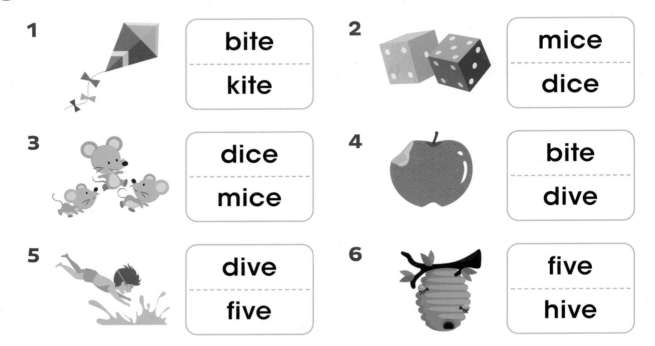

five

2

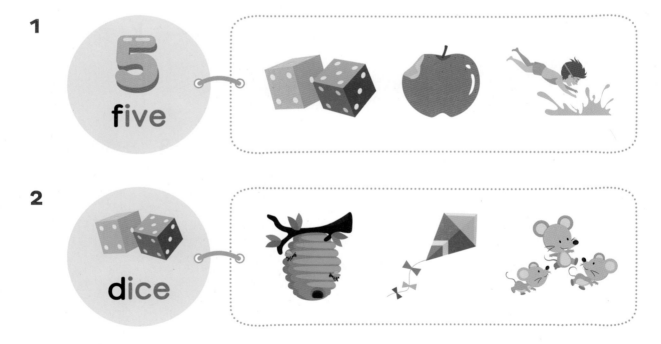

dice

C Write and match.

1

m_ _ _ _

4

b_ _ _ _

2

f_ _ _ _

5

d_ _ _ _

3

k_ _ _ _

6

d_ _ _ _

D Find and circle.

1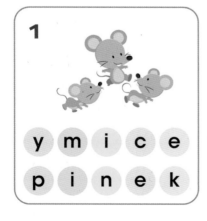

y m i c e
p i n e k

2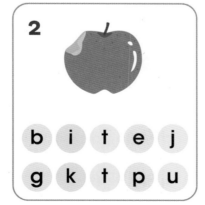

b i t e j
g k t p u

3

c b i k e
x h i v e

Check and write.

1

☐ -ice
☐ -ive

2

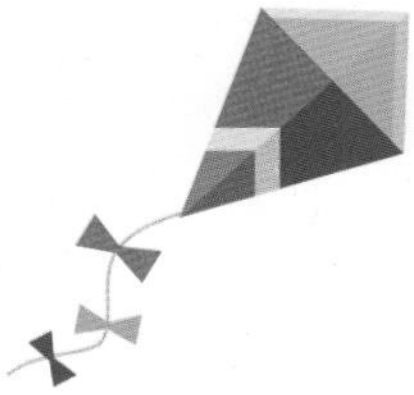

☐ -ice
☐ -ite

3

☐ -ive
☐ -ice

4

☐ -ite
☐ -ive

5

☐ -ite
☐ -ice

6

☐ -ive
☐ -ite

7

☐ -ite
☐ -ice

F **Find, circle, and write.**

t	q	b	i	t	e	q	z
w	i	p	c	f	m	i	c
q	h	v	i	i	a	j	f
g	w	y	y	v	s	r	l
d	k	i	t	e	e	x	t
i	i	q	m	i	c	e	d
v	w	c	s	n	y	u	f
e	r	c	e	y	f	p	s

1 -ice

mice

_____

2 -ite

_____

3 -ive

_____

A Look and match.

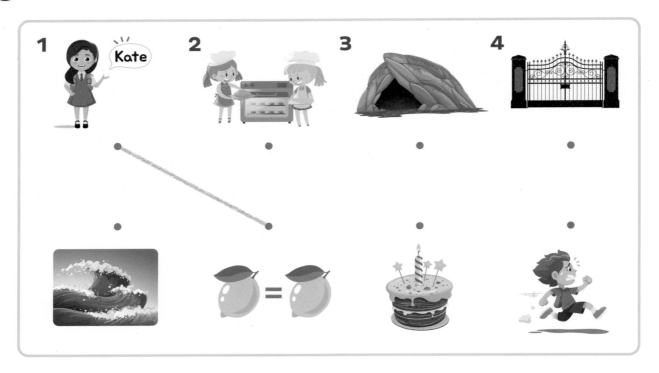

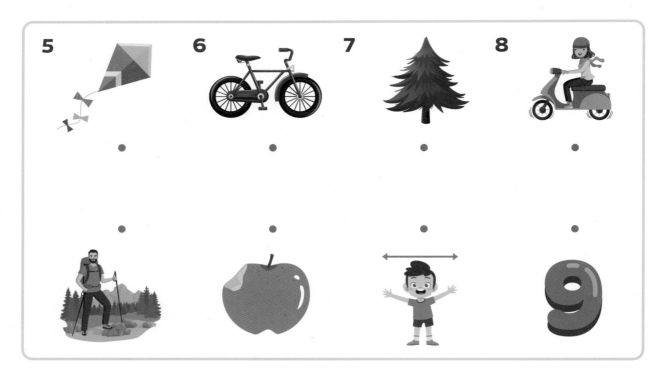

B Find and circle the long a words. Then read.

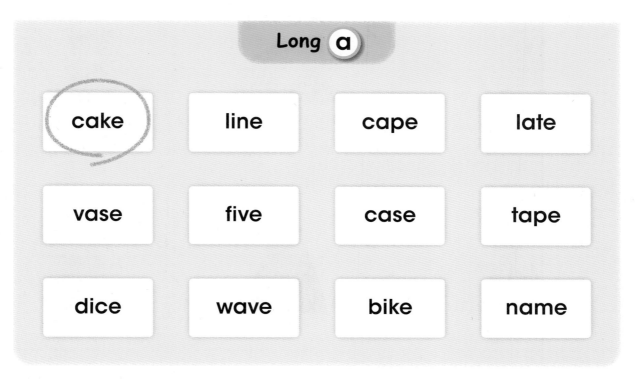

Long **a**

cake	line	cape	late
vase	five	case	tape
dice	wave	bike	name

C Find and circle the long i words. Then read.

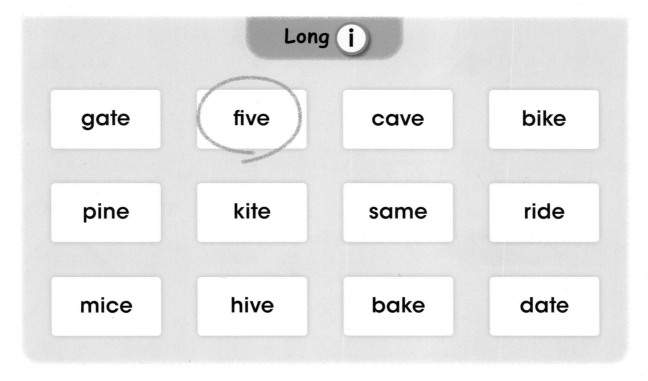

Long **i**

gate	five	cave	bike
pine	kite	same	ride
mice	hive	bake	date

D Write the words.

1

lake

2

3

4

5

6

7

8

9

10

11

12

E Look, unscramble, and write.

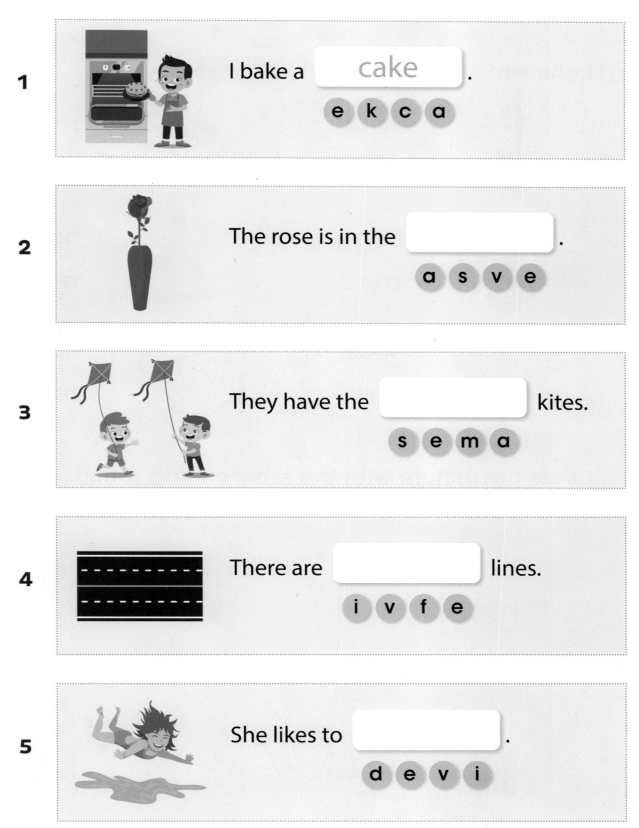

1. I bake a [cake] .

   e k c a

2. The rose is in the [_____] .

   a s v e

3. They have the [_____] kites.

   s e m a

4. There are [_____] lines.

   i v f e

5. She likes to [_____] .

   d e v i

A Look and circle.

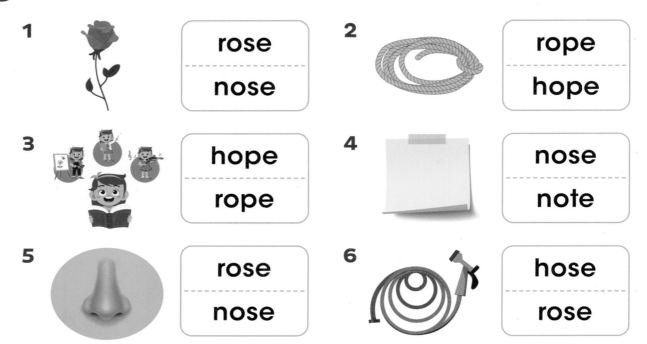

1. rose / nose
2. rope / hope
3. hope / rope
4. nose / note
5. rose / nose
6. hose / rose

B Circle the picture with the same ending sounds.

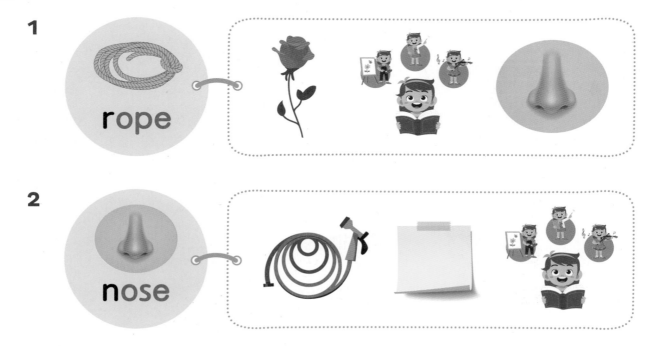

1. rope

2. nose

C Look and circle.

1

ote

2

ose

3

ose

4

ope

D Write and match.

1

r_____ _____ _____

3

r_____ _____ _____

2

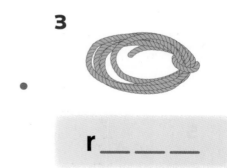

h_____ _____ _____

4

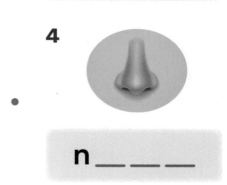

n_____ _____ _____

E Check and write.

1

□ -ope

□ -ose

2

□ -ote

□ -ose

3

□ -ose

□ -ope

4

□ -ose

□ -ote

5

□ -ope

□ -ose

6

□ -ote

□ -ope

F **Find, circle, and write.**

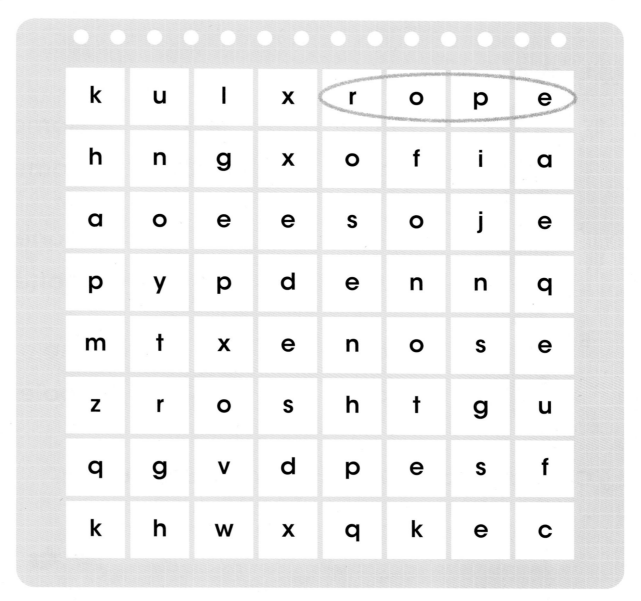

k	u	l	x	r	o	p	e
h	n	g	x	o	f	i	a
a	o	e	e	s	o	j	e
p	y	p	d	e	n	n	q
m	t	x	e	n	o	s	e
z	r	o	s	h	t	g	u
q	g	v	d	p	e	s	f
k	h	w	x	q	k	e	c

1 **-ope**

rope

2 **-ose**

3 **-ote**

A Look and circle.

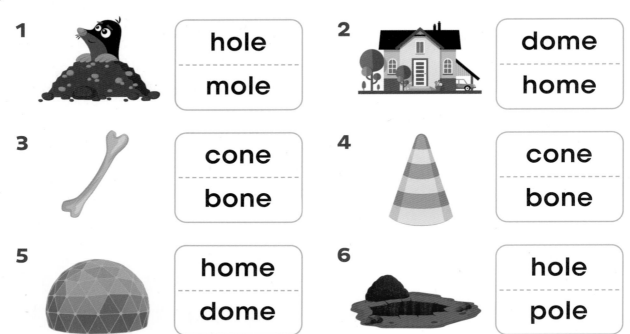

1 hole
mole

2 dome
home

3 cone
bone

4 cone
bone

5 home
dome

6 hole
pole

B Circle the picture with the same ending sounds.

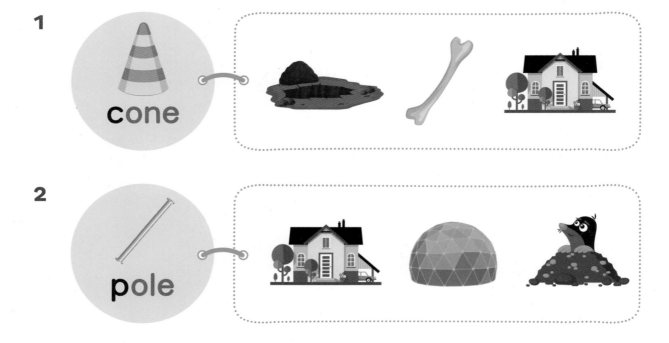

1 cone

2 pole

C Write and match.

1

d__ __ __

2

m__ __ __

3

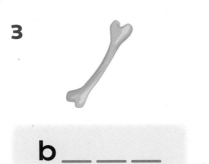

b__ __ __

4

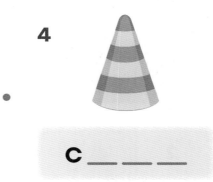

c__ __ __

5

h__ __ __

6

p__ __ __

D Find and circle.

1

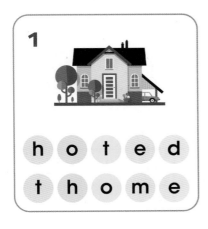

| h | o | t | e | d |
| t | h | o | m | e |

2

| d | h | o | l | e |
| o | p | l | w | i |

3

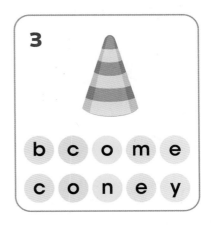

| b | c | o | m | e |
| c | o | n | e | y |

E Check and write.

1.
   - ☐ -one
   - ☐ -ome

2.
   - ☐ -ole
   - ☐ -one

3.
   - ☐ -ome
   - ☐ -ole

4.
   - ☐ -one
   - ☐ -ome

5.
   - ☐ -one
   - ☐ -ole

6.
   - ☐ -ome
   - ☐ -one

7.
   - ☐ -ole
   - ☐ -ome

F Find, circle, and write.

u	p	y	h	n	d	r	b
h	o	n	o	o	a	e	b
c	l	a	l	s	m	n	f
c	e	o	e	h	i	e	j
d	o	m	e	o	p	s	e
p	n	n	m	a	l	k	u
e	i	t	e	b	o	n	e
q	l	g	p	y	s	d	x

1 -ole

pole

2 -ome

3 -one

A Look and circle.

1

cube
tube

2

cute
mute

3

mute
flute

4

tune
tube

5

June
tune

6

flute
mute

B Circle the picture with the same ending sounds.

1

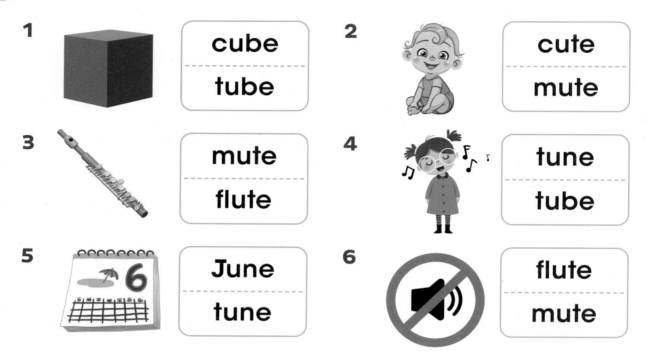

2

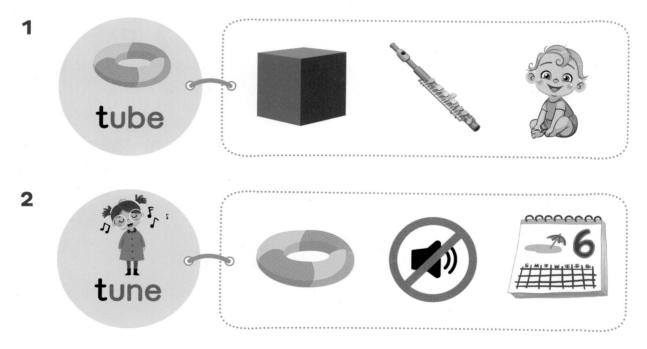

C Write and match.

1

m_____

2

t_____

3

c_____

4

J_____

5

t_____

6

c_____

D Find and circle.

1

a　s　g　k　e
s　t　u　b　e

2

b　c　u　t　e
g　h　c　u　b

3

t　u　n　e　f
u　i　r　e　b

E Check and write.

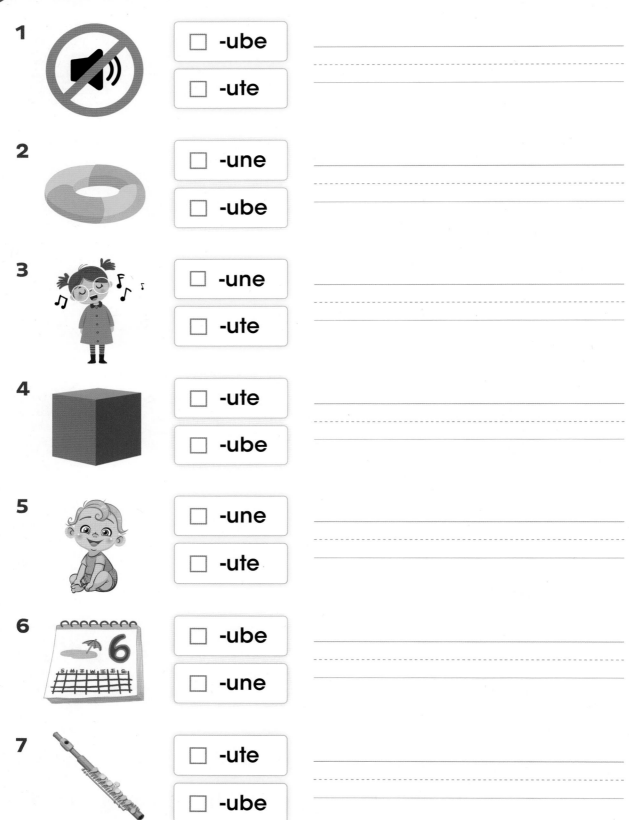

1. ☐ -ube ☐ -ute

2. ☐ -une ☐ -ube

3. ☐ -une ☐ -ute

4. ☐ -ute ☐ -ube

5. ☐ -une ☐ -ute

6. ☐ -ube ☐ -une

7. ☐ -ute ☐ -ube

F Find, circle, and write.

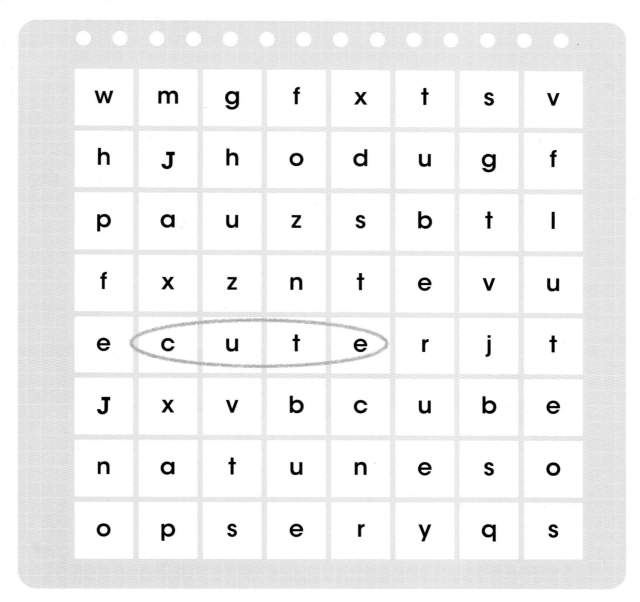

w	m	g	f	x	t	s	v
h	J	h	o	d	u	g	f
p	a	u	z	s	b	t	l
f	x	z	n	t	e	v	u
e	c	u	t	e	r	j	t
J	x	v	b	c	u	b	e
n	a	t	u	n	e	s	o
o	p	s	e	r	y	q	s

1 -ute

cute

2 -une

3 -ube

A Look and match.

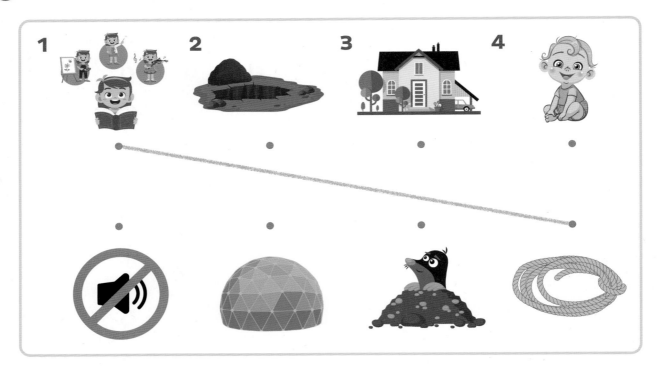

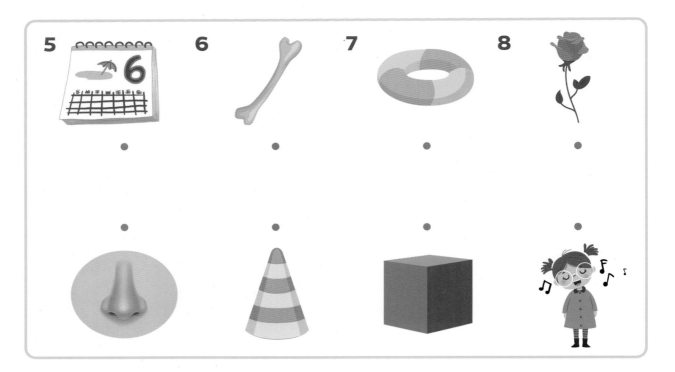

B Find and circle the long o words. Then read.

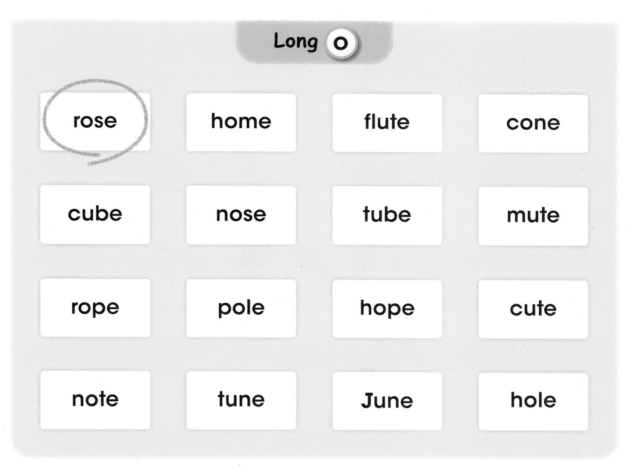

Long **o**

(rose)	home	flute	cone
cube	nose	tube	mute
rope	pole	hope	cute
note	tune	June	hole

C Find and circle the long u words. Then read.

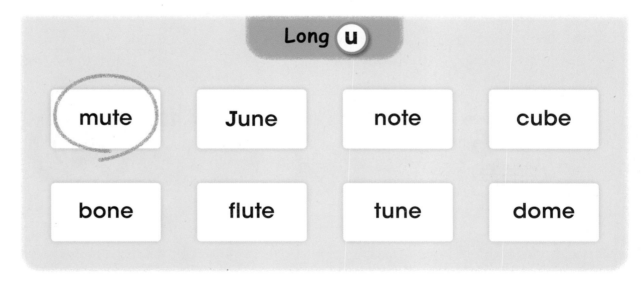

Long **u**

(mute)	June	note	cube
bone	flute	tune	dome

1

hose

2

3

4

5

6

7

8

9

10

11

12

E Look, unscramble, and write.

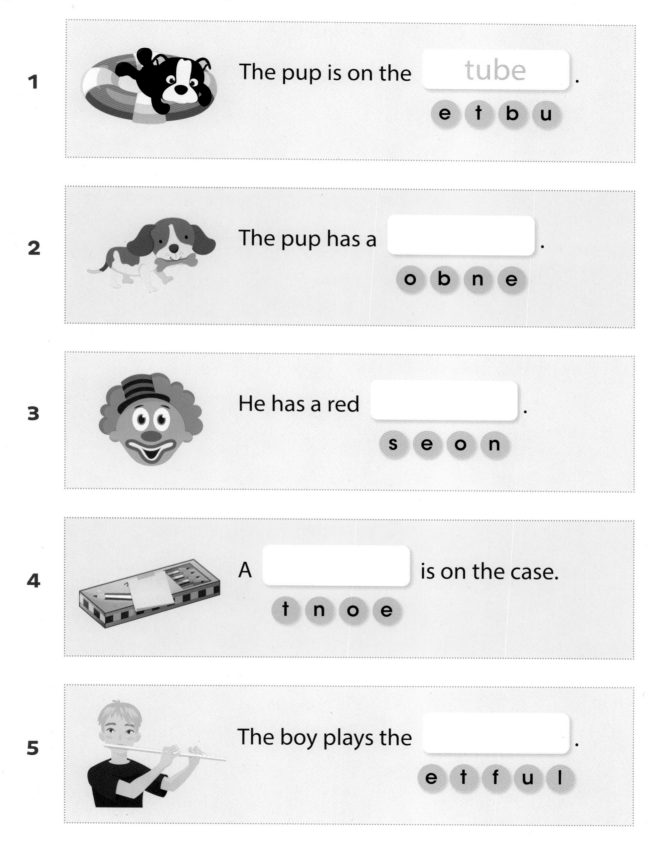

1 The pup is on the [tube].
   e t b u

2 The pup has a _____.
   o b n e

3 He has a red _____.
   s e o n

4 A _____ is on the case.
   t n o e

5 The boy plays the _____.
   e t f u l

Oh! My Phonics is a four-level series of phonics books designed for EFL students to help them learn the fundamentals of phonics with efficient and practical methods. This series greatly assists young learners in understanding the relationship between letters and sounds effectively and adequately. *Oh! My Phonics* also introduces a number of common sight words embedded in fun phonics stories. In this way, children can naturally improve their sight word reading skills.

Oh! My Phonics Series

Alphabet Sounds

Short Vowels

Long Vowels

Double Letters

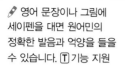

영어 문장이나 그림에 세이펜을 대면 원어민의 정확한 발음과 억양을 들을 수 있습니다. Ⓣ 기능 지원

스토리에 등장한 각 Sight Word에 세이펜을 대면 원어민의 정확한 발음을 들을 수 있습니다.

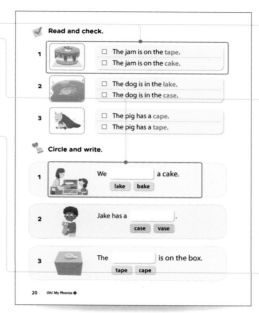

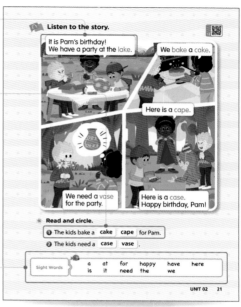

Listening 활동의 문제 번호에 펜을 대면 해당 문항의 음원이 재생됩니다.

각 단어나 그림에 세이펜을 대면 원어민의 정확한 발음과 억양을 들을 수 있습니다. Ⓣ 기능 지원

각 글자에 세이펜을 대면 원어민의 정확한 발음을 들을 수 있습니다.

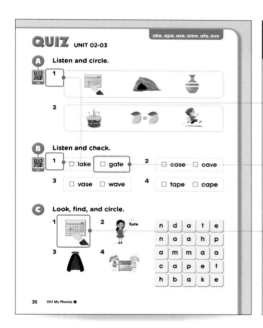

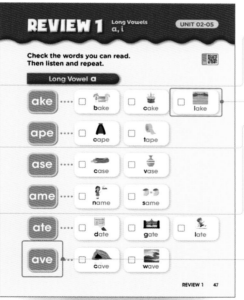

플래시카드의 각 단어나 그림에 세이펜을 대면 원어민의 정확한 발음과 억양을 들을 수 있습니다. Ⓣ 기능 지원

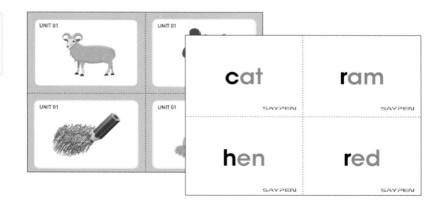

초등코치 천일문과
세이펜의 만남!

초등코치 천일문 시리즈 ✕ 세이펜 학습의 장점

01	02	03	04	05
녹음기능을 활용하여 발음 교정 및 쉐도잉 학습 가능	112개 대표 패턴 및 모든 문장을 원어민 발음으로 실시간 재생	게임모드를 활용한 즐거운 영어학습 가능	Role play를 이용한 가상 대화 체험 (Sentence에 한함)	이해하기 어려운 문법적 내용을 쉬운 해설과 함께 바로듣기 가능 (Grammar에 한함)

* 〈초등코치 천일문 시리즈〉는 세이펜이 적용된 도서입니다.
  세이펜을 영어에 가져다 대기만 하면 원어민이 들려주는 생생한 영어 발음과 억양을 바로 확인할 수 있습니다.

* 세이펜은 본 교재에 포함되어 있지 않습니다. 기존에 보유하신 세이펜이 있다면 핀파일만 다운로드해서 바로 이용하실 수 있습니다.
  단, Role-Play 기능은 SBS-1000 이후 모델에서만 구동됩니다.